The Suns Snow

And The Sands Move

A thing of magic from C. JoyBell C.

A special mention of the gifted artist "R. DC. G." for creating the C. JoyBell C. emblem used as cover art for this book. The emblem was materialized for the person of the author, and its worldwide Copyright remains solely with her.

"Cover art photo of author taken by Milan photographer Francesca Petringa in the Port Of Venus (Portovenere), Italy."

www.cjoybellc.com

 Dedication

I dedicate this book to my beloved son, Gilead. And I
bequeath these writings unto every soul that is on the
wild, raw, savage journey of becoming human. Also,
to those of you who are growing wings!

There is some kind of a sweet innocence in being

human— in not having to be just happy or just sad—

in the nature of being able to be both broken and

whole, at the same time.

Revelation

I am like a diamond
Born to the earth
The years have covered me in
Grime and mud
Filth and stench
Dirt and dung
But now is today and
I will dance and dance
I will dance and dance
I will dance and dance
I will dance and watch the dirt fall off
I will dance and watch the mud crack
And drop
I will dance and all the filth and grime
Will float away into the air
And I will see myself again
And so will you

Human

Toppled down
And all that's left
Is the me
That's hidden
Beneath these waves
Behind this sun
Under the blanket
Of these stars
I am hidden
And now
All is toppled down
I stand bare
A soul
That's raw
My strength exceeds me
My heart feels
When all is toppled down
The walls are down
I bleed emotion
Stay with me
Touch me
Walk with me

Talk to me
Keep me
From drowning
Under these waves
Keep me
From burning
Inside this sun
Keep me
From being forgotten
Under the blanket of these stars
Without you
I am not
Toppled down
Without you
I am hidden
Stay
Topple me down
Stay
Touch me
Stay
Walk with me
Stay
Talk to me
Keep me
From being hidden

Keep the heavens
From reclaiming me
The heavens
They want me
For their own
Stay
Keep me
Human

The Sun Is Snowing

Eyes translucent
Like the sun

Eyes transparent
Like the snowflakes

From beyond my skin

Inside

The sun is snowing

Transcendence

I am being pulled into me
Like a rogue wave called by
The voice of Jupiter into the sky;
Sprouts wings of foamy water
And flies into the Heavens,
To quench the thirst of his moons!

I am falling from my own skin
Forming into my existence
Like the drops of sea escaping
The mouth of Poseidon
Dripping down his chin
I have shed my skin

Until I am become nothing other
Than me Than I

And into this new wind I will go
Given new eyes with the transcendence
Of the Larimar
I smell no scent of my old skin

But only the scent of me
Like before the day I was born

Like before a fell, before I was fallen
Now I am free Now I am me

Today Is Forever

Today
the sunlight shines from places
eternal.

From places this world does not know.
From places
eternal.

Today
the sun rises on the shores of
the death of time,

on the horizons of
forever and
ever.

Today my body thinks it's dead.

Because my spirit soars too high.

The Becoming

I will break this clay jar
Until every drop of the incense inside
Will flow out of my soul and
Into my veins
And mix and swim in my bloodstream

And I will smell only like it
Every inch of me
Until I am unrecognizable
Until I have become me

When The Angels...

She fell from the heavens
On a dark night
When the angels sighed
With their breaths of
Faith and Hope and Love

Onto a castle in the dark
Of night she cascaded
Down amongst the stars
Falling, landing, resting on
The castle gate of limestone

In the Ligurian Sea

In the dark.
When the angels sighed.

The Princess

I tell you a tale
Come from a time long ago.
And from a place
That only I know.
A place and a time that
I come from; a place
From the magics of old!

There once was a soul,
The soul of a girl; from the
Brightest stardusts she was made!
From the dusts of Alcyone
One of the seven sisters
In Pleiades there she was formed!

Into her God breathed life
And called her "Alnair" (the bright)
For a true princess
That she would be!
Gifted with the brave heart of
Monoceros and the winged soul of
Altair, a real and true princess was she!

On the back of Pegasus
She descended to earth
And was one day born a girl.
Every mountain she climbed, every
Dark valley walked
Dared her forget who she was!

She learned bravery from the lambs,
Faith from the soft voices
She learned love and care
From a stone.
With what she had;
From this she made glad;
Unshakeable and trustworthy was she!

For the princesses of today
Are not princesses at all!
A princess is never naïve nor weak!
Nay! Though blessed with the angels' face,
And all of the angels' grace;
Unmovable in valor she should be!

Though they dared her forget
Her own heart, her own soul; Alnair
Faltered not in the end!
She toppled beasts and fought witches
From the stead of her throne
The throne which her soul
Sat upon!

For your enemies can never make you
Who you are not
And darkness can never make you forget!
You who are born a princess
With the angels' face and all of their grace
And inside you lies a true hero's heart!

The Candles

A beautiful dream comes to me
From the Heavens, the magics of old
My dream descends upon me
Melting onto my mind
Caressing my heart
Like sweet incense
Soothingly
Melting
Like butter onto my skin
In my dream
The candles- they are singing!
In the darkness I watch them- singing!
Tall grandfathers with heavy and thick
Melted wax dripping down cloaking them grandly
like
Long white beards they
Laugh and sing proudly!
Passing their little flame
They light the little children
Small and stout the little ones
Are gleeful
And joyful

They jump
Up and down and they
Reach for the flame
The grandfathers pass
Around and
The women too
They gladly lift their voices
A choir are they!
The most beautiful choir
I have ever heard
My tears fall down
To hear their voices
Their voices like bells
At Christmastime
The choir
The laugh
They pass
On the light and they sing
Their flame is upon
Each one of them now
And the grandfathers
The women the children
They sing
In harmony
For me

They bring me love and
They comfort my soul
They sing to my soul
They love and they comfort me
My pain
Is gone
Gone away
And the candles they sing for me
And I watch
And I listen
And I feel
And the candles they mend my soul

My beautiful dream
Of the candles they
Sing to me
In the dark
And I awake
And I am healed
My soul is here
My soul is mended
The pain is gone
And I am whole

The beautiful candles

Their beautiful song
Like Christmas bells
They sing to me

The candles that came
To heal my soul

Indulgence

I have no choice but to
Indulge my senses completely

Falling into you Rolling into you
Like tides on the ocean's shore

The Journey

Sometimes, the dreams that you dreamt never forget you, even long after you have forgotten them! You are little, your heart full of courage, and you dream dreams. You breathe life into visions you have of yourself, you look into the skies at night, out of your window, and as you breathe you breathe life into these pictures you've painted in the air and onto the tablets of your heart! Then you grow up, and slowly but surely the bravery takes flight from your spirit and you lose courage. You forget your dreams, you lose the pictures you painted and once carried with you.

But what takes us so long to realize, is that the dreams we breathed to life continued on! It is only us who forgot them but when we gave them life, they went on living.

And then they find us again one day, our dreams find us and they still recognize us! Even if the courage is gone, we are broken in places, shattered here and there; when our visions find us they still remember us and then they remind us, of a courage we once had! Of places we once visited in our hearts once upon a starry night. And then we remember. And then we sojourn, we go out on our journeys. We walk with our dreams. And during this time, we find ourselves!

Ten Thousand Seagulls

(June 9, 2010 ~ Roma, Italia)

Basilica bells ring
Waking the city of Roma
The Roman alley:
Small bags of trash
Contrast the beauty of
Wooden Italian shutters
And wrought iron terraces!
Small yellow lights beam
And glow from within
"Ciao" and they kiss
On both cheeks
Ten thousand seagulls
Roam the skies
Like white sailboats
Sailing upon the Heavens
"Kaw kaw kaaaawwww" they resound
Beautiful like bells they sing
The seagulls, a promise of beauty
Swans of the skies
The Basilica bells, a promise of
Eternity
I breathe in your eternal air

Your eternal flame:
I think I felt it flicker
In my heart!
"Ciao" and they kiss
On both cheeks
"Papa" calls the small boy
"Amore" answers papa
And then I think
Then
(The flicker in my soul,
My heart filled)
I have found what I
Have been looking for

It's Amore!

(June 11, 2010 ~ Roma, Italia)

It is possible to fall in love
But how is it possible
To fall in love with a city?

For I have fallen in love
Today and yesterday and
The day before yesterday!

I have fallen in love every
Day since I have gotten here
Over and over and over again.

I have fallen in love
Fallen in love fallen in love
I have fallen in love with Roma

Piazza di Spagna

(June 13, 2010 ~ Roma, Italia)

Step by step and
One by one they
Ascend they descend like
Ladders to the gods
The mortals take shield
Us mortals take refuge
Loitering these divine steps
Sitting, laying, kneeling, sprawling
Red roses dance ballet
Chilly air Hot sun
Lovers kissing Children laughing
Sounds of life abound
And here I am
History under my feet
I drink in the
Sounds of life and
Sounds of love and
Chilly air Hot sun

Piazza di Spagna

Walking The Streets Of Roma

(June 13, 2010~ Roma, Italia)

I feel this stone under
My feet and I think
I feel the thousand years gone by
Seeping through the bottoms
Of my shoes
Up and down the
Stone-laden streets
My shoes are not used to this
Nor are my feet
Mini-palaces painted with
Pastel cherubims
Angels bump their shoulders together
They share each others' skin
Basilica bells chime
Old priests nod and smile
At me
I breathe in the air
That Caesar, Da Vinci, Leonardo, Michelangelo
And about a hundred
Great popes breathed
Ancient history fills my lungs
I exhale aged art

Antiquated thoughts
Timeless souls
The yellow flowers climb on walls
The man sits with his Afghan Hound
Lovers loiter the air I breathe
With their kisses
And sighs of *amore!*
I feel the stones
From beneath my shoes
They go "bump-bump" on the
Bottoms of my feet
Stones placed by makers of
Rennaisance art and
Primordial love and
Thousands- of- years- old history
Porcelain dolls
In flower-lined windows,
Wooden Pinocchios,
Carvings of fat women,
And white-winged equines;
Call to me as I walk by!
I hear someone making love
From a window in a
Gellateria!
Could I ever ask for more in life

XXVI

Than walking the streets of Roma?

Ponte Vecchio

(July 27, 2010 ~ Firenze, Italia)

She spreads herself over the
Top of the arched bridge way
And flutters her green, blue, brown
Window shutters
And so seductively has she cast
Herself over the water for man to see,
Perchance it feels like I am beholding
A promiscuous woman
Who flutters her eyelids in the
Wind and
Over the waters
To capture the attention of men
And when you enter her
She will offer you
Balconies of gold
White Yellow Rose
Gold
Terraces of diamonds
Princess Round Square
Cut diamonds
Dens of pearls
White Grey Black

XXVIII

Pearls

Drawing you in

She will tempt you with her

Many offers

And lure you with her

Sounds of irreplaceable music

Flowing from her sidewalks

An offering for the ears

And you are poisoned

And you...

You have become hers

The oil paintings

On the cobblestone

Swim for your eyes

You are intoxicated

The rusted locks

Forever locked

Names of lovers

Locked in love

And you are taken

None is of you

You have become hers

The Ponte Vecchio

The Pigeons

Come and gone Come and gone
Sun has risen Rain has fallen
Burns on my back Scorchings of the ages
Scars of summers come Forgings of winters gone
My skin glistening Marble reflecting this daylight
They come and go Come and go
These pigeons they land and Fly they fly away
Here today Gone tomorrow
And I will always Always I will be here
Bearing summer Braving winters
Constant Constant Constant Constant
Constant Constant Constant Constant
I am a pledge A carving in stone
The statue The statue of marble
Wars have begun Wars have ended
Old blood once spilled New life now born
The sky it is running Fast across above me
Gray and white White and gray
The bells are ringing The sky is racing
And I watch And I see
And I wait And I love
The sky it moves My breath breathed into me

XXX

They always come Come and go
It is always come Come and gone
And I am here I am still here
If you stop If you stop to look at me
Then you might You might then see me
And stay with me Stay and not fly away…
The pigeons they always The pigeons are always
landing
They land and fly They land then fly away

Effervescent

From under the maroon cloak of envy's breath
From beneath the airless blanket of oppression's wing
From behind the shadow of injustice
From inside the belly of desperation
Her light still soaks through
Like white wine through cotton
Her warmth is still felt
Like radiating embers
Her effervescence is still seen
Like the reflection of the moon
Or amber sunlit on an afternoon
She still swells with glory
Illuminating further into the horizon
Brighter than all of them put together!

Unstoppable

Walk On This Water

To strike this strong current with my oar
Is the only thought I hold in sight

To rage against the falling of this flow
Is the only force that hands this oar

Rage rage Strike and rage
South it falls and North I follow

How long must I rage
How far must I strike

This river forces downwards
But I fight on upwards

My strength; it is aching
I will throw my oar away; and instead

I will walk
On this water

XXXIII

The Twenty Thousand

About twenty thousand
Divided into four
All at my right hand
On the grey ocean shore

Golden horses leap
With knights on their backs
Statues come to life
They breathe as I pass

O'er the blue-grey stones I tread
The sky grey as the shore
Captured by the cold beneath my feet
The smooth stones; weathered but unworn

Five thousand golden horses
Suddenly they leap
Five thousand grounded warriors
Alas! They lift their feet!

Five thousand great rocks
Breathing soldiers they've become!

Five thousand bronze statues
Together lift their swords!

The sky a still blue-grey
Reflected on the waters
The stones beneath my feet
Licked by the frosty vapors

Here beyond the great door
The great door that I opened
I breathe life to something ancient
Ancient and long-forgotten

About twenty thousand soldiers
Divided into four
And the golden horses
Awaited me on these shores

And now they breathe

Their hearts are beating

To where they go

I don't know

XXXV

Restoration

Her screams resound
On galaxies
They race between
The stars
Her anguished wails
Of pained longings
Rip
Through the solar systems
Below and beyond and above
The demons cower
The angels stand still
Her cries tear
Asunder
The rulers of
A thousand planets
Hide behind
Their thrones and temples
She calls through the Heavens
A heartbreaking command
The light pulsates
From the galaxies
"Give me back what is mine!

Now give it all back to me!
I want what is mine!
What is mine give back to me!"
She grabs the moon
And throws it
With a vengeance
She destroys the white moons
All lined up in a long row
A semi-circle
She crushes them
With every thrust
The white moons are nothing
But white dust
She raises her face to the above
Her head tossed back
In pangs of anguish
Her screams heard through
The universe
The soles of her feet float
Over the pond
The pond of the window
To everything else
"I want to go home!
Give me what is mine!"
The demons see their death draw nigh

And to her small
Plateau of columns
And pillars
She goes; pain in every stride
There she looks
To left and to right
Her spirit blazing
Ablaze in her eyes
The angels stand still
They wait from afar
She clasps the pillars
She grabs on
To these columns
And the lightning bolts
They are held back
In black clouds
The universe
Bows its head
And she screams

"Give me what is mine!"
Her voice like torture

So loud
So loud

XXXVIII

It echoes through

Beyond and
Beyond

"Give me all that is mine!
Give back to me all that is mine!"

The lifts the ailing stones in her hands
Places them one on top of the other
With the forgotten, trampled rocks
She tries to rebuild what once was

Venus wants her temple back

Something

It's something like
Suddenly red and
Blue beside the
Red and water
Swims all around
And the blue
And red together
They are sudden
Like something that
Makes me feel
Free and I
Want to swim
In the water
Droplets that skip
On the blue
And red its
Something like that
But
I don't know
What it is

Memories Of Turquoise

I remember the egg
Made of blue sapphire and amethysts
I remember the sea
Splitting into two
I recognize these walls of waters separating
These walls of waters opening
Leading underneath
I recall the high places in the deepest depths of the
Seas, *Neptunia prata*
The faint image of a mighty man
Threatens to recapture my memory
Did I run from him
With the egg of precious stone?
Or is it he who bequeathed me with this journey?
Did I fear him? This mighty man of the seas?
Or was he my father?
Did I flee from him in a flight of random terror?
Or was the egg of precious stone
My destiny? My journey?
A darkness overcame the shore, the land;
From this black day did I escape?
Or through this doom did I brave my flight?

Faint memories…
They glisten in my mind

Yellow Boulders

I want you to rush up
Into me warm like
The tides of the
Ligurian Sea

Lick the contours of my skin like
The afternoon waves will
Lick at the yellow boulders
Of Portovenere

The Status Of A Clam

The pirate fondles with his memories
And like air they drizzle in on
The winds sweeping his way from the
Nearby ports, bringing with it the smells
Of freshly caught fish, and these
Memories of ages past
Old and wrought like iron
Drift inwards like sunlight through the
Windows, softly murmuring along the off-white
Curtains
And there they are
With him now
Captured by his being
Like water pouring over him
The brutes the braves the sweet things
Of the past which now scramble
For their own permanence; their own existence
In this precious mind which slowly
But surely dwindles along with old age
Like clams that are caught up in
The ocean's tides, washed onto the seashore
And then taken back again into each

XLIV

Of their lonely statuses.

Sands of Time

The sands of my childhood are
Saturated in a fervent coral-tinted hue of peach
Glistening; each sand glistening under the *soleil*
Like twinkling stars; daughters of the day
Altogether bathed in waters of cyan blue
They cling together seamlessly and appear like
An endless blanket that is the shoreline
Cyan studs my footprints and leaps!
Like fleas: disappearing into the sand
To touch to touch to touch to touch to touch
This sand, *sorra*; to feel it through my fingers
This sand, *sorra*; to pick it up with my hand
This sand, *sorra*; to feel it in my palms

The sounds of the cyan against this shore

The voices that call me to leave and let go and come
in

No

XLVI

Here I will stay. On the peach coral sand. Beside the
blue.

To feel it.

And the sands of you are like that dream
The one that awakes me in light
The dream that is so bright that it awakes me in it's
light
And then washes me while I smile
I smile because I feel you
Sands under the white light of always and always
The existence between time and space and knowing
But I know
And these sands they are drowned in the beauty of
this light
To soak to soak to stay to stay to breathe
This light, this air, this *sorra*
This *sorra*; falling over me
This *sorra*; infiltrating me
This sand; steals my sleep and awakes me
Somewhere else

Somewhere I want to be

XLVII

And I feel the voices of the awake and they move
around

But I will be awakened only in this light. And smile.
This sand.

Is where I want to be.

The Differents

The photographs lined his wall
A woman
A beautiful smile
Captures of joy
Trappings of love
He walked out and I said
"you still love her"
Pain stung the air and
I wish I hadn't said it
He looked down
To the ground
I didn't even know him
Not even his name

I touched her shoulder and
I watched her eyes dilate
Her fears run away
Peace overcame her
She didn't even know me
Not even my name

I felt that tear fall

Falling rolling on my skin
But it's not my own
It fell
A thousand miles away
It's not mine
But it falls on my skin

I looked into his eyes
I recognized him
From a different time
I welcomed his soul
His soul walked into mine
Again

I'm glowing
They all say I'm glowing

I needed sunlight and
The sunlight came into place

In agony I lifted my face
To the Heavens and
Clouds of gray were born

I was sitting on the sidewalk when

L

He came up to me and said
"you are different, very different"
He didn't even know me

If he only knew how different

Hell

They said to me "speak"
When I spoke they struck my face

They said "show us your hand"
And my hand they then cut off

They said to me "stand up"
And then they cut me down

Today I am in hell
Because I did all that they said

Goodbye Paper Birds

Do you see this window?
This window that I see now?

From this window I can see them
I can see them on the inside

I can see them on the inside
From the outside I look in

There is a place I once knew
Therein they still are

They still sit behind that window
They still live inside that room

Paper castles hang on the walls
sway in the window

Cardboard forts stand neatly arranged
Cardboard hearts stuck on the boxes

They are at home

They have made their answers

They have made their answers
They crossed-out all their questions

In the room lays carton coffins
Headstones made from cut-outs

They write out their days
They spell out their end

I am on the outside
On the outside looking in

Up here the winds speed high
The winds expand my wings

I'm flying

The stars hang in front of me
The world looks like a marble

My path is made of water
I am walking on water

This flight has just begun
Only the winds know where I'm going

The waters are changing
The lights are breathing

The borders are lined up
They mean nothing to me

My questions are not answered
My end is nonexistent

All is given to me
I have no walls for paper castles

From the outside I look in
I know those people well

We used to share those windows
I hung some birds there made of paper

So far, far, far, far away…
So far, far, far, far away…

Goodbye.

LV

The God With Eyes That Have No Colour

I have many brothers and sisters. My brothers are white and my sisters are black. I have many cousins, aunts, and uncles. My cousins are yellow, my aunts are brown, and my uncles are red. I have many mothers and fathers. My mothers are caramel and my fathers are orange. This is my family. We may not share the same blood, but we share the same air that we breathe! We may not go to the same church, but we are all created by the same God. You are my brother. You are my sister. You are my cousin. You are my uncle. You are my aunt. You are my mother. You are my father. We live by the same air. The children of one God.

Come out! Crawl out! Run out! Emerge from beneath the rocks! Disassemble from inside those caves! Disembark from your heavily-laden ships! You yellow man! You red man! Straighten your backs! Lift your torsos upward-bound! Let your voices ring freely towards the skies! You black man! You white man! Run and pick up speed! Fly and abound on new heights! Soar, feel the winds through your feathers! You brown man! You orange man! You man of caramel-coloured skin!

Quiver like the string in the tight-stretched bow! And then let go! Pierce the bull's eye! Quiver! Quiver! Shake and quiver! For the power within you is great! And then fly!

Imprint. Emerge. Sculpt your face in the winds! You human of many colours! Sculpt your image! Carve it into the air for eternity's heritage! You human who is not bound and bridled by one borderline! You human who is not traced in by lines drawn onto the map!

I eat the countries' borders drawn neatly on the map! I pick them up and they slither together as a thing of no form! I bury the limits of man into the sands to watch them slowly die.

You man of many colors! Arise! Unfold your wings! The wings of the Phoenix! And burn your name into the skies of before, of here, and of after and evermore! Burn your name and may it be burned into the air in many colours! And may your colours be your legacy for the coloured eyes of mankind to see! And may God our creator look at you and see – a beautiful flight of fiery dancing wings aflame etching the skies! And may God feel this heat. The God of eyes that have no colour! May your colours burn and He feel the warmth against His face!

Changing Everything

Along you came
I saw you stumbling
Through the door
The sun was shining
From behind you
The crooked smile on your face
Made the sun
Shine brighter
Along you came
I thought I'd never
See that sun again
But along you came
The crooked smile on your face
Made the sun
Shine even brighter
I thought I'd never
Unlock that door again
The sky is still and blue
Behind you
You cast a soft shadow
On the floor
Your smile is crooked

Your crooked smile
Puts me back together again
Your crooked smile
Makes all the roads look straight
Again
You can stay
And lock the door behind you
We can throw away the key
I'll open the windows
The sunlight will flood in
And the sun will shine brighter behind you
The sky will be
Still
And blue
Above us
Your crooked smile
Will make the walls
Look straight
Again
I was the only
Crooked thing
Until...
Your crooked, crooked self came in...
Let's sneak out
The back door

LX

Let's take a walk
Down the beaten road
Your crooked smile
Will set it straight
Again
Your crooked self
Will find me

Ours. Forever.

I don't think we're in our boat anymore.

Nomore black waves.
Nomore vicious storms.
Nomore sea monsters.

I see we've reached our shore of solid gold.

Our immoveable foundation.
Our untouchable strength.
Our indestructible ground.

And on our golden shore we are one through and
through.

One breath shared.
One heartbeat shared.
One spirit shared.

And as we stand as one we look in front of us.

A still breeze.

A steady calm.
A formidable peace.

Ours. Forever.

Impassioned

Must I
Forever
Be plagued
With passions?
Passions
Which engulf
And drown
Me
Why has God gifted me
With a heart
That feels too much?
More than anything
I feel too much
Of this
Of that
Must I go on this way
Forever?
Plagued with
Lusts for everything?
Lusts for faith
Lusts for love
Lusts for joy

A lust of

Simply breathing

Overcome am I

My own skin cannot contain me

I sit

And eat the world

Out of the palm of my hand

This heart…

Impassioned…

This heart is impassioned

My own skin cannot contain me

Can anything contain me?

I think not.

Why have I

Been gifted

With a heart

That eats the world

And all that's in it?

Shall I burn

Like hot fire

For eternity?

Am I to swim

Out

To the horizons

The horizons of everything…

For forever?
For day and night
I swim
To the edges of everything
And I never
Even want
To come back!

My Only Love

I will take him by the hands
His hands in mine
I will lead him
And I will show him all the wonders of me

I will be wonderful to him
Slowly I will show him the way
I will bring him to my garden
And I will show him all the wonders of me

As we walk I will face him
And while he looks at me
I will look into his eyes
And I will show him all the wonders of me

Slowly my wings will unfold
While budding in the sunlight they will unfold
My wings will twinkle and sparkle for him
And I will show him all the wonders of me

The grass beneath my feet will come to life
With every step my feet will bring life

LXVII

Under my footsteps the grass will take root
And I will show him all the wonders of me

With each brush of the hem of my dress
With each touch of the edge of my garments
The daisies will blossom the flowers will bloom
And I will show him all the wonders of me

Slowly we walk
My eyes take him in
Sunbeams dance on our faces
And I will show him all the wonders of me

My wings brush the leaves
The tips of my wings wash over the leaves
With every touch the cherries blossom
And I will show him all the wonders of me

Deeper and deeper into my hideaway
Further and further into my garden
Where unicorns roam and faeries dance
And I will show him all the wonders of me

The meadow is come alive
There is life all around us

LXVIII

The deer skips the butterflies flutter the ladybug
crawls
And I will show him all the wonders of me

Sunlight bathes my hair
His heart makes me smile
I look into his eyes
And I will show him all the wonders of me

He will play with the deer he will merry with the
lambs
He will reach for the cherries the peaches and the
berries
He will drink from the stream the stream that flows
freely
And I will show him all the wonders of me

Deeper and deeper
Farther and farther
Into the meadows
We are now running

The faeries they dance
The harps play their music
The roses blossom

Underneath our touch

Our laughter is wild
Our song reaches to the heavens
We call on the angels
With our song

Day turns to night
The night is enchanted
The moonlight tastes sweet
Like honey

Magic is real
We make our own magic
Clothed in moonlight
Cloaked under magic

The night turns to morning
Our eyelids wet with dew
The scent of the meadow
Poisons our hair

The morning is aglow
The dewdrops sparkle
Under sunbeams

LXX

Two hearts beat as one

The roses they have bloomed
The cherries they have blossomed
The grass the meadow the stream
All is alive

All is still in the softness of the morning

I will turn to him and his skin will touch mine
I will hold him close and lay my head on his chest
He is mine and I am all his
The garden is ours the meadow is our own

And I will show him all the wonders of me.

Me

Wait for me
and I will come to you with the sunlight *llum del sol*.

Wait for me
and I will embrace you with its yellow glow.

Wait for me
and I will flood over your skin with the sun's rays.

Wait for me
and I will pull you in with the sun's light by moon.

Wait for me
and I will come upon you in the mornings- soft and
white like a dove.

Wait for me
and I will enter your soul- yellow and deep like gold.

Wait for me
and I will be only yours.

The Window, My Soul, The Sun, The Sea

There is a window I see, which I can

jump out of.

And as I fall, I don't really fall,

but I arrive…

at a place eternal. A place

that I knew, that I know, that always

will call to me.

The sea of the sun is vast like a vastness

I have never seen before. I do not have to try

not to sink on the sun. The blue is deep

and it is not-so-soft and it

holds my soul together

LXXIII

as I float and at the sun's horizon

is where the clouds meet the sun's

halo and the halo touches the sea...

and I float...and my soul swells...

held together by the tides of the ocean.

It is only me who is here. But I am

not lonely. Nor am I alone.

My soul held together by the tides

of the ocean on the eternal *sol*. And when

I look up....

I can see the window...

Not Two (Just One)

In and out
of each other we go;

like the sun's rays filter
through the raindrops.

I can fondle your soul
and you can cradle mine.

I see through your pupils,
like a breath exhaled into the air.

You see what I see,
I see what you see.

Where do you begin?
Where do I end?

Where do I begin?
Where do you end?

Playful like pure joy,

we filter through each other.

Like light filters through the heavens.
Our vision is one.

We are not two. We are just one.

I See You

From over the seas
From beyond your own patch of stars
My heart
Will teach you
From the other side
Of the horizon
From beyond
Your own mountain range
My heart
Will talk to you
On the waves that no ship
Can sail
My heart will bring
My whispers to you
Through the valleys that no wagon
Can fit through
My heart will skip with song
And sing my songs
To you
From where you cannot see me
My heart
Sees you

LXXVII

My heart

Feels you

I will

Teach you

To see me

To feel me

Too

My heart will teach you

Have faith

In yourself

All of my faith

Is in you

I see you

With my heart

I feel you

With my heart

I place all

My faith in you

For my faith

Has now found a home

In you

My heart has found

A home for my faith

And it has brought

My faith to you

LXXVIII

My heart…

I…

I will teach you

To see me

My heart…

I…

I will teach you

To see yourself

How I see you

I see you

With a whole heart of faith

From across the distance

My heart

Will teach you

To see

You

Too

Mischievous, Delinquent, Conqueror

The sunlight plays
Hide and seek with
Me
Behind the windows
It curls
Tentatively it hides
I can almost hear
Its mischievous laughter
As it teases my eyes, my skin;
On top of it
The warmth dances
The mischief of the
Sunlight
Playing games with my
Senses

The moderate breezes of
Midday bump into each other
In midair
Teasing the tips of my hair
Scampering along the edge of
My brow like

Delinquent children running and
Skipping in the streets

The mischievous sunlight and
The delinquent breeze

But the teasing sunshine is
Captured by
The golden tassels of the
Curtains
Lightly tingling in the breeze
Shivering like they are cold and
Freezing in a winter wind
Captured by the golden tassels
The sunshine is not as free as
It thinks it is

Golden isles
Like golden isles off the coasts
Of the Mediterranean seas
I spot the sunbeams
Caught by the tassels

The mischievous sunlight and
The delinquent breeze and

LXXXI

The conquering tassels

At the edge of my curtains

Empath

A piece of a soul
All covered in blue
I picked up by a stream
A steady stone pathing my way

A part of a soul
All warm like sunshine
Shimmered and blazed like light
Just behind the waterfall
Guiding my way like
A torch in the night

A pocketful of a soul
Clear and wishful
Like midday
Swims around me like air
Through to the mountaintops
It leads my way
Ascending

Pieces of a puzzle
A puzzle I make my bridgeway

LXXXIII

My bridgeway of steel, wood, and rope
Steady leading the way o'er
The waterfalls
To the other side

Pieces of a puzzle
A puzzle I make my pathway
My pathway of stone, brick, and tar
Steady providing my tread o'er
The forest moss-grounds
Through the woods thick

Pieces of a puzzle
Feelings that I see
Are whispers in my ear
Are voices calling me

Invisible Happenings

As your ship sails
Away into the
Misty horizon
Silent whispers
Go with it
Into the night like
Invisible happenings
I see them like
Ghosts that once
Laughed and skipped
With me but now
Turn their backs
On me
The ghosts fade away
Into the overcast horizon
They follow your ship

I am beginning to forget
That I once
Was there
Sailing your ship
With you

LXXXV

Magic

The flames leap at ancient stones
Enchanted flames burn the color of amber
Burn with enchantment
Dance on the flames with me

The flames leap at ancient stones
Enchanted flames burn the color of amber
Burn with enchantment
Dance on the flames with me

The flames leap at ancient stones
Enchanted flames burn the color of amber
Burn with enchantment
Dance on the flames with me

He Is The Same

My thoughts have turned to the ways of God
I have found myself pondering upon His mercies
His mercies are new as the dew every morning
His steadfastness is still and everlasting
His steadfastness like the sunrise

I am thinking of the ways or our God
The paths He sets are ones of truth
Many a choice He has set before us
Freedom He holds in each hand
Freedom is the wind that picks up His wings

My soul is softened when I remember the ways of my
God
He has brought me out and set me forth
Laden with every good thing; I have been
Offered with all good gifts; I always am
I doubt not; I fear not the intentions of my God

He is steadfast in all His ways
My God is the beginning; only He is the end
Time and space can bear no judgments against me

LXXXVII

My God has held me up high in His right hand
Even the science of time and space pay their homage
to me

For this is my God; he is a good God
His tender mercies and loving kindness…
…they continue to dance upon time
Throughout all generations
He is the same

Raw Nudity

Raw
Nude
Angels

Lesser
Than
God

Higher
Than
Man

I Do Not

I
do not
hang
like a
dewdrop
at the
end
of the
silk
thread of
mercy.

Roman Trains And Traffic

(June 9, 2010 ~ Roma, Italia)

Run! Run!

Hurry! Hurry!

Get out of my way!

In a flight

Of random wits!

Outwit the Roman

Trains and traffic

Were those train tracks

I just ran past?

I think I almost

Got run over

By a mini scooter!

The Snowflake

(For my friend, Net de Ubago de Andrade
and her lost snowflake, Chloe.)

A petal…
A rose…
From heaven
Silently it falls
Onto your life
Touching you
With its tender
Caress
Then just as soon as
You feel it on your
Skin
It's gone
A snowflake…
A single flake of snow…
From heaven
Silently it falls
Onto your life
Touching you
With its tender
Promises

Then just as soon as
You feel it on your
Skin
It's gone
A raindrop...
The rain...
From heaven
Silently it falls
Onto your life
Touching you
With its tender
Feelings
Then just as soon as
You feel it on your
Skin
It's gone
Oh god in heaven
Why do you bless us
With a caress
With a promise
With a feeling
If they are
To flutter away
To melt away
To disappear

Oh God…
My God…
Show me where
The roses bloom
In thousands
Manifold
Show me where
The snowflakes gather
In the mountains
Far untold
Show me where
The raindrops form
Wells lakes rivers oceans
Where do they unfold?
God…
Give me back my baby…
Her soul to me
Bring back
I am humbled
That I pray
The ground may have her body
But her soul
To me
Bring back

XCIV

Fuchsia

"I want it to have a three-sisters skirt
Three layers long and flowing"
I remember how I told you and
Then you told the dressmaker
And how she drew a sketch
Onto the paper by the sewing machine
"I want it to be this color"
"That's fuchsia" you said
I ran my fingers over the shiny
Fuchsia cloth
I remember how it made me happy
"I want it to have round puffy sleeves
And pink crepe roses stuck onto it"
I told you and you told the dressmaker
By her sewing machine at the Dress Shoppe
My shoes were too big and
I couldn't walk in high heels
The tiara was too big, too.
But my fuchsia dress was perfect
In all our pictures we were happy
This dress was my dream and
We both made it come to life

XCV

Together
I know that we don't have much
To remember
But fuchsia makes me happy
And we made this together
Ma
It was the time right before
We stopped being happy

Winter Bloom

She's a single winter bloom, a single bloom in the winter, the only thing of color, a single precious life blossoming in the cold, cold snow. And all around her it is lifeless, lifeless and cold. But all her colors against the stark, white *neve* seem to make it all better; seem to make the harsh winter okay.

Sometimes when I touch her, she's frozen. Her petals are frosted and icy to the core. Her stem suspended into a life-like etch against the background snow. And her leaves… her leaves become as brittle as the things around her. But still, still she is rooted and still she alone makes the picture so lovely. She never looses her color.

When the sun comes out, it shines for her. Warms her until her heart beats again. Sunbeams tilt her head up towards the warm sky. And the sun shines for her. Just for her.

Sometimes I feel
like a winter bloom.
A scarlet rose
in the dead of winter.

The Shining Little

The angel sits over the city
Brightly colored lights sing from down below
From the other side of the window
And here as she oversees the coming
And going of the celestial tides
Evident in the clouds just slightly
Above the tops of the building which
Graze the Heavens
Her thoughts can be seen in her eyes
Playing for you like film flickering before
Her pupils
Her wounded arm that bled last night
Now heals as her weary body finds
Solitude and healing in the comforts of
Twilight
And the brightly colored lights from
Down below bounce upon the
Thoughts running through her irises like
Christmas candle flames on a
Crystal mirror
When you embrace her when you see her
She will enter your soul and she will

Become your life your blood
And she will never ever leave you
When you run away when you walk away
She will take you to the coldest mountain peeks
And watch your soul burn in sudden freezing
Leaving you there to die, to fall
Tired is she of the fires that seize her
Burdened is she by the torrents that freeze her
Now with her arm cut but healing
Her magenta blood spilled last night she sees
Now like a movie playing on
The walls of her memory she sees
They are only afraid
They only do not understand
They simply do not know
Their own hearts they do not see
She is too big for them they
Scamper back to where they came from
Like frightened creatures of the night
These humans
They do not know
They run away
And though her heart breaks to be
Left and rejected time and time
Again she knows the truth now:

C

No one has really rejected her
It is only very hard
To meet an angel
She runs her finger gently over the
Wound jagged through her arm
Down to her elbow it runs to
Remind her that
She is not like them
But if it is not possible to have
Someone who will stay and keep her
Human
Like the warm permanence of the
Lights that dot airport runways at night
Usurping permanence of times that
Are both a beginning and a goodbye
They encompass all limits of time
Yet in such a simple way just by being there
Wouldn't it be nice
To have someone to look at her
And say
"She is not very big nor very dangerous at all. In fact,
She is quite little.
But alas…
She is only very, very shiny."

The Error of Mortal Men

The only problem with her is that she is too perfect. She is bad in a way that entices, and good in a way that comforts. She is mischief but then she is the warmth of home. The dreams of the wild and dangerous but the memories of childhood and gladness. She is perfection. And when given something perfect, it is the nature of man to dedicate his mind to finding something wrong with it and then when he is able to find something wrong with it, he rejoices in his find, and sees only the flaw, becoming blind to everything else! And this is why man is never given anything that is perfect, because when given the imperfect and the ugly, man will dedicate his mind to finding what is good with the imperfect and upon finding one thing good with the extremely flawed, he will see only the one good thing, and no longer see everything that is ugly! And so...man complains to God for having less than what he wants... but this is the only thing that man can handle! Man cannot handle what is perfect. It is the nature of the mortal to rejoice over the single thing that he can proudly say he found on his own, with no help from another; whether it be a shadow in a perfect diamond, or a faint beautiful reflection in an extremely dull mirror!

This is the great error of mortal men.

Diamonds and Skulls

This world is a vast land scattered with dead bodies, vultures, betrayal, hyenas, greed, poison, injustice, scorpions, mirages, and parched, dehydrated ground. The heat scorches the skin on your back, and your walk feels endless and aimless. But then. He who lives is he who sees the lilies growing in between the dried bones, she who lives is she who walks beside the unseen and endless flow of turquoise water that streamlines continuously through, you live if you can watch the bubbling fountains springing up in between the corpses and the rot and the stench. In this world, hideous as it may be, you live when you can dwell in the overlooked, when you can thrive on the unseen, if you can find joy in the rose of Sharon blooming amongst the forgotten bones, if you can find joy in the lily of the valley budding amongst the ghosts, if you can fathom the water lily floating in a steamy sky; in the absence of water! We live if we can see the dusty diamonds lying beneath the skulls then roll those skeletons away and take those diamonds.

Unbridled

The explorer lifts her lamp up unto her face
The shadows of her perfect silhouette bounce
And dance upon the suede walls and
Archaic stones polished and rubbed to
Appear new again.
Leading the way she lifts her light unto
Her beautiful face
So fragile So unafraid
And as these billowy shadows leap and chant
Like the very intentions of her own heart and
The flames of her lamp warm up the air
"There is no need to tame me"
And the flame crackled and licked the glass
Walls of it's little containment
"If I am to love you may it beknownst
That I am to love you with all of
Mine own heart and all of my own
Mind untamed as it is; untamed as
I am and may my love not be
Born of a result of masterminding,
Trickery, schemes, and manipulation lest I
Look upon that love and disrespect

It for I do not want to belong
To you tamed and relinquished;
That to me is an end of what
Love is for what is a love if not
That which is the overcoming of
One's existence and the thrusting of this
In full force with all of the burning
Passions of one's desires
And you act as if though you want
To tame me
I am too much for any such sort of
A thing as that which you speak of
And I will love you but I will love you
Because I want to love you and not
Because I have been bridled and saddled and whipped
And if this is not the sort of love that you
Desire then I should think that it is only
For the reason that you are not man enough to have
me"

She always looked you straight in the eye
Standing upright in full spirit; one that
Could never be broken.

Αλφα *and* Ωμέγα

I see it I feel it
Rushing towards me over the
Peaceful rage of the sea
As my feet sink into the
Sands of this shore
The Αλφα and Ωμέγα
Speaks to me
That is His voice
I see it I feel it
The very existence of it
Pulls the matter of the air
And space and rips through
The skies and through time
And overcomes the presence of
The living waves beneath it
Over the midnight deep of
The ocean and cutting through
The violet and magenta of the air
The Αλφα and Ωμέγα speaks to me
His voice comes to me
Like the rippling and bubbling of
The seafoam dancing over my skin

His voice heals me
His voice comforts me
He is with me
The Αλφα and Ωμέγα

Daughter of Zeus

At the feet of Zeus on Oros Olympos
Stood a single blue rose

"Why do you cry, blue rose?" asked Zeus.
"Because I am not made of nature!" said blue rose.
"Why do you bleed, blue rose?" asked Zeus.
"Because they value what is made of nature more
than what is not!" said the blue rose.
"Blue rose, do you not know, that what is not made
by nature, is made by the hands of the gods?
Blue rose, do you not know, that what does not exist
in nature, *is* the *blood* of the gods?
And do you not know, that splendor is not found in
numbers? Is a field of daisies more eminent than a
single blue rose?" her father Zeus answered.

"But they don't understand!"

"We do not exist to be understood; we exist because
we are."

The Storm

The skies are impregnated
With grayness, death, and life
Life giving waters that fall from a gray sky
Having the power to wash away homes
And memories, lives, and treasures
It is when this dark impregnation takes place
That I am given a deep visual
A peace about the past
An assurance about the future
These gray winds
Sway me to sleep
These gray skies
Sing me into peace
And though the burden of devastation
Mounts onto the back of this storm
And I have felt sorrow
For the oppressed
With this death also comes life
A mirror washed clean again
A new beginning
A definite end
A fresh journey

A closed door
This storm is the *perfect balance*

Home

When I look into the grey skies
Pregnant with rain and thunder
I feel as though I am in the company of many
I feel as though my brothers and my sisters
Call to me
I would come home to a hearty feast, a laden banquet
If I could fly into the dark skies, and step into those
clouds!

When I am covered in sunlight
When I feel the tugging warmth of the sun against
my skin
I feel as though I am found again
I feel as though my mother and my father
Comfort me
And in the sun's embrace I recall
All of my cherished memories, and the beautiful
moments…

Always

I have this vision of myself.

The night is deep and the stars are many.

My heart swells and shines.

And with my fingertip, I reach out
just a little
and touch each star in front of me.

And one by one they meet my fingertip.

My skin.

And I am smiling; I reach out
just a little
and touch the stars in front of me.

And it feels like…I have always been here.

Nightingale

Peace lives inside me

And from inside me

It calls with a voice

With it's voice it calls

Like the nightingale

With The Equines

Even the wind that gushed against my skin
Echoed the freedom of their souls
As we ran together
Wild and unstoppable

Even faster than they
I ran on the wind
Laughing in the spirit of pure wildness
Laughter that shook my soul

And vibrated just beneath my skin:

Eating me
Devouring me
Dissolving me
Creating me

The wind itself was composed of
This equine spirit
Unbridled, unbound
I flew through it

Free

Soaring above the horses just below me
I mingled with them
I ran
And I flew

My spirit leaped in the air
And reached for the sun

We flew together, we ran together

When I Found Me

I was just about to
Give up on me when
I saw me step out from
Behind the secret places
And into the bright
Visions where I stay

Where the sun is snowing

And then I saw my
Face with the light
Falling and drifting
Gently off of my skin
And floating out into
The air and all around
Me and then
I remembered me

Eyes translucent like the sun
Eyes transparent like the snowflakes

It is okay to shine

CXVII

The Coming Of The Water Lilies

White water lilies
They float on an
Aquamarine sky
Casting reflections upon my eyes
Like the mirror image of leaves
Swaying and drifting over lakes
In the amber Autumn

These reflections softly float above me
Like answers to my questions
Like guardians of my soul
And I wait for
The coming of the water lilies

Pleiades

From the dust of the heavenly stars I was molded by the hands of God. With the stardust of Pleiades God formed me. Born of the dust of the earth here I am; in the quest to find true love abiding in a pure heart.

In the lights of Alcyone my soul took its first breath. On the pearls of Monoceros my spirit first mounted in flight. In the golden caves of Polaris my heart's desire was formed (to have true love abiding in a pure heart has since been my wish).

On the wings of Pegasus I found not my heart's content. Feasting at the tables of Mira I ate not my fill. Hiding myself in the brightness of Hyades I knew not my safety.

And here now- here I am- my body born of earthly dust; I have come to this place on my journey to a thousand stars. On this quest to find true love abiding in a pure heart. I search amongst the mortals' souls.

Here is where I will find true love living and thriving in the soul of a mortal man. Radiant and sweet within his pure heart- life to my spirit, food for my soul. The journey to a thousand stars is nearing its end.

The Blue House

I see the little blue house on a hill
At night in my dreams, I see it over
And over again; night after night and

I remember this house
But it was not blue

But here in my dreams
It is blue and
It is haunted

The blue house in my dreams is haunted
By my memories of love and oneness
Haunted by the ghosts of what was once
My own

The ghosts they feel

So near
So near

But they are so far away

CXXI

Living in my blue house on the hill

That I remember
Wasn't really blue but
In my dreams is always blue

Last night there was an earthquake
And the haunted house fell down

CXXII

Eagle

The grey morning mists
Curl on the sides of my face
Up here in the clouds
On the mountaintops
My spirit soars like the eagle!

The cool air consumes my soul
In release in freedom
I go beyond all my former fears
Sailing over the mountaintops
My spirit soars like the eagle!

On feathered wings I tilt
At the sun's angle through
The sky and my eye
Catches the rays of sunlight *llum del sol*
My spirit soars like the eagle!

My face to heaven raises
Catching the gaze of God and angel
The beat of my wings chant in
Melodious humming, breaking the air

My spirit soars like the eagle!

Lightning and thunder be
Captured in my eyes like
Prints of the memories of Heaven
Stamped onto my soul; and I take flight!
My spirit soars like the eagle

Goodbye

Throw

Your

Worries

Into

The

Mirror

And

Let

Them

Go

Off

Into

Other

Worlds

Faith

I look and I see
The narrow path on which I have tread
The narrow path winding the side of this mountain
This mountain that reaches high into the clouds
Over cliffs of rock and jagged stone
This path curves and winds and dances
A path so narrow that my shoulder against the stone
Has constantly pushed me off to the edge
To the edge, to the end, to the brink of death
If I were to fall from walking this precarious path
Surely my death I would meet
And through the mist and the fog and the clouds
I cannot see beyond myself as I travel these steps
Upwards they wind
Always upward, around the cliffs of this mountain
A continuous winding, turning
I am the pilgrim of this path
I am the martyr of these steps
I am the saint of this mountain
Upwards and always upwards is my route
I cannot see beyond myself but I can feel another
mountain to my side

CXXVI

And this is why I do not fall
Into an abyss
Into a dessert valley
For I feel I am in between two mountains
From the one I am pushed, for the path is too narrow
But onto the other I lean and I am steadied
I have walked this path for many a long stride!
Many a year, many a morrow!
And I have reached the mountaintop!
Now from this mountain I shall fly!
I can spread my wings and can you see, I have flown!
Through the clouds
From above through the clouds I peer down
To find the other mountain I could not see

But there is none

There was no second mountain
There is only a deep abyss
There is only the unknown drop
There is only the fall, the valley
Down below
Low low low down below
There is nothing but emptiness
And death

CXXVII

I never fell because
I believed
That something would never let me

The Brotherhood Of The Fathers

Let us go yonder
Beyond our own seas and valleys
Past our ports and trading steads
To the distant towns and those peculiar peoples

Let us tear down their pagan temples
Dismantle their altars stone by stone
Desecrate their steps and pedestals
We will bring to naught their holy of holies

Let us build our sanctuaries on their sacred
foundations
We will tell them that we are their redemption
Their salvation, the forgiveness of their sins
We will give them to shame

Banish them!
Enslave them!
Cast these people out!

Let us garnish them as sinners
As nothing more than savage

CXXIX

Lesser ones to be forgotten
Dismissed ignorant barbarians

Let us confine the gods to myth and legend
Stories for the children
Tall tales, lies, imagery!
Nothing more than simple amusements

Then let us carefully remove the statues
The sculptures of Zeus
Those figures of Venus
This replica of Poseidon

Then let us bind the gods to us
Here with us, in our chambers!
Under our roof, within our walls!
We will break bread in their presence!

Then let us emulsify in the glory
Of the imprints of the gods
Their thoughts bent always towards us
Captured in their images

We are their sanctuary now!
We are their new foundation!

CXXX

We will bind and harness the gods!

And let us fear not
For there will be none to come and free them
Their peoples have been silenced
In their own fear of sin and accusation

And let us sleep well
The world cannot remember them
They are only bedtime stories
There is none to fear but us

Us alone

Find Me in the Dusk

How sweet is this twilight,
That it has brought whispers to my ears?

How vital is the tug of light and dark,
That it has pulled me out of myself?

In these hours my soul is honored
During these volatile minutes, my spirit is enthroned

Like a fast seagull through the space
Between a maroon sky and glassy sea, *Neptunia Prata*

I engage in the sprint of life,
And these few, free, ambrosial hedonisms!

If you look for me where the
Light meets the darkness

You will find me.

Animalistic

The veins in his arms
Protruded right below the
Very surface of his skin
And a faint hue of scarlet
spread itself slowly—
his flesh washed in warmth.
Bound by his skin
Were shapely muscles
Tense and firm
I detected beads of sweat
Appear on his brow
Right along his hairline

The movement of your blood through your veins
The pulsating throb of your heart in your chest
The distributing warmth running through your flesh

It grabs me
It pulls me

And I can feel my own pulse beat faster
As if my own arteries share in your blood

CXXXIII

I can feel my forehead moisten with sweat
You'd think we were covered in the same skin

It was a humid summer afternoon
The day he walked into that place
I like to watch the heat of the sun
Work its wonders on
A red-blooded man

Sin-Like

I am involved in a romance
A deep, dark, bright, lit passionate romance
With life
What is life? It is the air I breathe?
The answers and the questions?
The paths that Destiny carved out in stone?
I will always walk with Destiny
And God; He whispers the answers into my ears
What is this romance? What makes it deep and dark
And bright and lit?
This is a love story: I am in love with the memories
of old
The sex of the ancients
To make a long, deep and dark love
Not only with my own existence
But to exchange essence with the breaths
And the sighs and the laughter and the thoughts
The love and the emancipation
Of a thousand others before me
Ten thousand more likely
This is the romance that I live

The Sirens' Song

Feed me the grapes from the golden bowl of Venus
Lest this night pass and my skin not touch the foam
Whistle to me waters, the song of many lovers
Bring to me waves, the grapes upon this sea

Feed me the grapes from the golden bowl of Venus
Spew the purple juice onto the brightest star
Catch the fallen prayers of Bellatrix and Zeta
Bring to me waves, the scaling skin of lovers' pray'rs

(This song is borrowed from the novel, *Dimensions* by C.
Joy-Bett C.)

Of Hope, Still

There is a bit of a hope still left
It is like a couple of vanilla sands
Crystallized and cut like diamonds
Undisturbed, peaking out from the
Dry crevices of a deserted dam

There is a small thing of hope, still.
It is like a seashell of coral-apricot tones
A surprise, a catching of the eyes
Barely surfacing for a breath of air
From under the forgotten sea foam

There is a glimpse of a reflection of this thing hope
It is like a very small pocket mirror
Catching the rays of the sun in reflections
Someone dropped the mirror and there it sits
Halfway covered and halfway exposed in the shore

Yes. There is a little hope left.

Venus

An apple tree planted in an orange grove will
Still bear apples
A swan born in the ducks' haven will
Still become beautiful
An eagle fallen into the cave of bats will
One day gain its sight

When God plants a blue rose
Red paint will wash away

Venus born to a man and a woman
Will still be risen by God, from the foam of Liguria

Inner Peace 2

She thought she had found peace before, until
She saw herself sitting here, afloat
On this tranquil solitude of water
Not a ripple, not a stir
Accompanies her here
On this motionless skin of water
Yet underneath, it's heart beats
And it flows and travels

And she thought that she had peace before
Until she found herself here in the crevice of
The ripped silk scarf of time
And she entered into the peace inside
The peace inside that passes all of any understanding
And she sat down and she floated
On this water's skin
Serenity and stillness beget this place of power

Peace is power

She touches her skin onto the surface of this water
A single finger reaches out

CXXXIX

To skim the top of this water
And it is only the sensation of her flesh
That this water needs to ripple

To whirl and to churn and to foam
And spit white horses
Just a single touch
The power to move the waters
Pushing mountains into seas

This is Inner Peace

My Hand In Yours

The surface of your skin

Your fingers

Gently

Slowly

Move over the surface

Of mine

Like a trickle of water

Down my thigh

The nerves in my body

Soothed

Warmed

My hand in yours

Makes my hand look

So small

So small

Your arms around

My waist

Possess me

Your arms enclosing around my waist

So tight

I could stop breathing

You want to never let go of me
You never want to let go of me

Stay

Eros

I am not going to
Sit and eat with
A little silver spoon
The love in front of me

I will only lift my
Bowl unto my face
And drown in my love
Until I have eaten it all

We Are The Angels

You make me
Nude
You make me
Brokendown

You eat my
Soul
My soul that's
Raw
There's no other
Me
But me that's
Raw

And burning

You pull me
Out
Out through my
Eyes

The day is

Dark
Days dark and
Evil

We soar in
Flight
Soaring through the
Darkness

I see the
Lightning
The reflections of
Lightning

In your eyes

And I feel
Thunder
Thunder here inside
Me

You make me
Thunder
You make me
Nude

Your palm in
Mine
Your hot palm
Sweats

Bound by the
Heavens
Sealed as burning
Lights

We are the angels

Blanket

Like the strands of flannel on my blanket
That cling onto my skin, I want to feel
You; pull you up in between me and
Have your warmth all over running inside
Me and contouring to the folds of my skin

Our Hands

My hand in yours
Your hand
Makes my hand
Look so small

Don't leave me

The scent of you
From behind my ear
Your arms around me
Your breath strong against my neck

Stay here

No one has ever
Held me so tight
Before
You want to never let me go

Keep me

You never want to let me go

CXLVIII

Your squeeze… so tight
I could stop breathing
I can feel your breathing

Don't let go of me

Inner Peace 1

Here I sit on the surface of this water
Deep and dark and still: this water

Here I float on the surface of this water
Motionless and serene and tranquil: this water

And I thought I knew peace before
Until I found myself immoveable here

And I thought I had peace before
Until I saw myself floating here

Floating, sitting, on the surface of this water
Not a ripple, not a stir

In my eyes
Inner Peace

Yet if I touch the top of this solitary river
With the tip of my finger

CL

I can create a whirlpool, a wave, a ripple!

If I only tap the skin of this water with my own skin
I will create a foaming swell of waves, white horses!

My power is abundant in this stillness
In this calm

Inside of me
Inner Peace

I am manifest in this silence
In this letting go

Losing My Religion

It has fallen off of my wrist
Like a golden bracelet
Inscribed with many promises
Incantations and spells
Hindering my existence
Clouding my sight, stifling my vision
Distorting my sense of smell, Disfiguring
And the hexed golden bracelet
Has fallen
It hits the marble floor like
A hammer on a chisel
All motion is still
Only the movement of the falling thing
Descending through the air with the sound of
Broken, falling chains
Ripping through the air gently
Shattering on the floor, Defeated

I have lost my religion

My Betrothal

What does it feel like?
It feels like an abandon
Of everything not needful
It feels like an encompassing
Waterfall revealing herself eternally

Given to serenity

The still lake The flowing river
The constant peace of
Undisturbed tides
In the day I am
The illuminated turquoise lake
By night I am
The moonlit water abandoning,
Descending from the rocks:
A beautiful abandon
An enlightenment of peace

Given to serenity

The river runs deep

A water unfathomable and immovable
But then it is light like the air
As it cascades like white wings
In the moonlight
Leaving behind that which is unnecessary
Forsaking
All the magnets that wish to hold
All the dams that stand to bind
Is it a reckless abandon?
An untamed, all-knowing look in the eyes?
Is it a sweetness, a wind beneath the wings?

Given to serenity

I have found a place
Wherein I will stay
These serene waters
A power beyond all powers
An abandon more real than most
In the heart of serenity

Leave everything behind

The Hymn of Klaus and Clyde

By the lily's shoreline
We sailed t'wards nile
The alabaster ladies soared
With the swans they glided
On the lake and downwards
Was the reflection of all heart
And lore, All heart and lore,
Don't forget the lily's shore
That sails t'wards the nile
The alabaster ladies, the
Winds on the wings
Of the swans

(This hymn is borrowed from the novel, Dimensions, by C.
Joy Bell C.)

Mermaid's Heart

Must I be concerned with you and those of your
likeness?
That I am to care about your downfall?
Did you not already know that I would drown you
and then eat you alive?
So why did you still cross my waters?
You did! You did know that it is my kind who drown
those like you
Who dare cross my seas
Evidently, you have still sailed
And perish
Is this to be of any concern of mine?
I fear not. I do not take responsibility and apologize
For the fate of you and your crew
When you knew plainly well where you were going
And what you were doing
When you crossed my waters
Destiny has dealt with you
I only dwell with Destiny; Venus has formed me
Am I damned? I doubt so.
Is it a sin to exist inside Destiny and with God?
Of course not

But only a fool sails a sea he knows will take him
Is it a fault of mine that I
Am placed within these waters?
Not so.
But it is your lack of understanding
That brought you here
No, I will not apologize for your fate!

The Truth About Poison

For a few of us, love and madness are the first things on our minds. Love is like a veil that lightly cascades over everything, and madness is a state of mind. We are the differents, and for the differents, no ordinary methods will do; no standard procedures are acceptable! Only a wild, otherworldly escapade of the soul will serve sufficient and anything less is simply unacceptable!

Therefore, how do we thrive in a world filled with those who do not even have a peripheral vision? They are all mundane and predictable, not overcome by any great thing! And look at us! We walk with Destiny, we think like madness, and we see through the eyes of a smoldering love! We watch people play in puddles while we rule the deepest oceans and seas!

We are an existence all our own: undiscovered and independent of the rest of the earth. We thrive only with the ones who are also like us, thus, it becomes a journey to find another different, another one like us!

There be many people who seek out love, who want to have love, who think that they are meant for love, but they live on the margins of the page; he who is not born a lover, will never really be a lover. You may find a romance, but if you are not born a lover, you will never know that great love they speak of. Lovers are born and reborn to one another, if you are not one of these, you will never have this. Yet you will have something else, something like a drunken stupor, something like a sweetened illusion. And if you really knew what it means to be born a lover, you would shut your mouth and drink of your own cup, contented, having quit wishing to be one!

We all think that we wish to have what is secret and what is truth in magic but the reality is, secrets are revealed to those who are able to speak with dragons, and truth in magic is given to those whose blood washes away poisons.

Flight

I have come to accept the feeling of not knowing where I am going. And I have trained myself to love it. Because it is only when we are suspended in mid-air with no landing in sight, that we force our wings to unravel and alas begin our flight. And as we fly, we still may not know where we are going to. But the miracle is in the unfolding of the wings. You may not know where you're going, but you know that so long as you spread your wings, the winds will carry you.

Flight is a very curious thing. It first terrifies you and the moment that it takes you is the moment that you have learned to love the feeling of complete dependency on the wind. On something you cannot see and you cannot hold. When we are afraid, we want to hold onto anything we can get our hands on. But I have come to understand that it is only when we let go of everything we are trying to hold onto; that we find what we are looking for. It is only on the winds that we can soar.

CLX

Almost

She has not even arrived yet
But from across the oceans
From beyond the Heavens and the skies
From over these deserts and times
Her spirit precedes her
And crushes all ogres along the way
Her spirit enlarges
And dismisses all hexes along the way
Her spirit is magnified
It demolishes all strongholds
Her spirit illuminates
It exposes all hiding place
And she is still only
On her way

Bothersome Tales And
Annoying Virtues

Tired of the bothersome
Virtues that bind; the
Tales of annoying virtues
That bind me; henceforth

I will no longer walk
By the tales of my mother
Along the straight and
Narrow path of timidity

And self-afflicted fears; so
Bottoms-up and all is well
Cheers, cheers and triple cheers
To the absence of virtue!

Cheers, cheers and
Triple cheers to the absence
Of all of mother's bothersome tales
And annoying virtues! Three cheers!

Bell

Warm, melodious
Conversations
That we
Haven't had
Yet
Chime
Like soft bells
In
My
Mind

I can hear them
Chiming now

A Disaster

Old wings dug up
New wings bestowed
Memories of lifetimes
Visions they unfold
Fear taking over
Guilt doubt and hate
Old wings flying higher
New wings broke down low

Your wings… why don't
they work anymore?

The Water Lilies Came

They float over this azure sky like paper boats
Sailing on cerulean waters
Quietly, they whisper my name
Their shadows hover over the ground
And I am beckoned unto my window to
Look up at the sky

Water lilies

They float together on the troposphere
Huddled together like a *mer* of swans
Over and above my head they float
Like meanings, healing, and answers birthed on
Mythical waters
The water lilies float

Vision

Light sheds
Falling off of my skin like
Gently drizzling snowflakes
The sun is snowing

Radiate

In sweet gentleness
My light radiates

My radiating light
Will protect me

My protection comes
From my brightness

My effervescent soul
Dispels all darkness

A Little Wonderful

I feel like I am

a little wonderful.

In this

whole, whole
big, big
horrible, horrible
world!

And there I am-

a little wonderful.

Irreverent

Something happened
Last night
While I was fast asleep
For when I awoke
This morning
Your shadow hovered
Over me no longer
Something must have happened
In my dreams
Last night
For this morn when I awoke
You
Like a second skin fallen-off
Lingered no more
Above me
I wonder what must have
Happened
As I lay me down
Last night
For today
I am no longer
Afraid

For today

My eyes are no longer

Overcast

For today

No black crow no red cardinal

Flies above me

Now

I smile a shining irreverent smile

Now

My eyes-they sparkle

Now

Nothing flies above me

Above me

Is only

The blue sky

Tonight

There will be white stars

Tomorrow

I will see the sun rise

For me

All for me

I am

A little love bird

With a string tied to my foot

For too long

In my dreams last night
The string was cut
And now
Now…
Irreverent…
And you
You…
Fly no more
Above me
Yes you are still there
Yes I see you still
But you fly above me
No more

Feathers

It will be okay
When you return to you
To the you who
Was there
Before the floods came
Before the castle toppled down
Before the earth shook, quaked

It will be okay
It will be silent
Serene
When you find yourself standing there
In the same place where you left
You

When you wonder if it's okay
To go and take your hand
To touch your face
And look into your eyes again
And find you,

You will see

CLXXII

That you have found
The place where feathers rain
And the Qilin tramples
Not even a single
Blade of grass

And your heart
Breaks not
Does not crack

Go back. It's okay.

The Woman In The Sunlight

Today I watched a woman walk beneath the
Sun's rays
I watched her for a few seconds
The strands of hair on her head illuminated under the
noontime sun like Swarovski under a bulb
The deep lines around her mouth introduced me to
Her former youth, her wedding day, the birth of her
first child (and the second and the third)
The engraved creases in her dark olive skin told me a
story of her many laughters, happy moments
I watched small shadows sneak their way underneath
strands of her wind-rustled bangs
The evident lines on her forehead welcomed me into
her home and
I heard her crying that day when he left her, I saw
her sorrow the time she thought she was forgotten!
The wind blew sunlight over her face, pushing aside
invisible curtains so I
Could see herself emerge as she strode down the
lane; Her bone structure looked emulsified in
determination and confidence
A face molded, sculpted by the hands of

Memory and Venture
Sort of a satisfying sensation tingled over my skin
Ah, to smell all the scents of a beautiful soul exhaled
to me in the wind!

She Who Still Dreams

I see a woman with dreams
Her head is held high,
her gaze straightforward.
She is petite
But
In all of her littleness
She raises herself up towards the sky
And occupies
All of herself that there is to be!
Her gestures are sure
Her stride; nothing special
but it is her own! Her own
walk into the world every day!

That's how I know she has dreams.

That's how I know she still dreams.

CLXXVI

White Shoes

(For my beloved son, Gil.)

I really feel that
Our love
Is like no other

And if I were
To compare
It to anything else

. . .

Our love is like
The rain
On warm summer afternoons

This love is like
The sun
On chilly winter mornings

You and me are
The answer
To many thoughtful questions

My love for you
The alabaster
On these ancient leathers

Your love for me
White shoes
Down these ordin'ry roads

The Italian Pizzeria

The Pizzeria
Tucked away
Painted yellow
And rust red
Chairs and tables
Dance on the alleys
Of the Italian
Pizzeria

Like Sweet Incense

a
deep
settled
intensely
sweet
passion

Undone

Like

Threads

Falling

In

Slow

Motion

Onto

The

Ground

I

Come

Undone

For

You

Swimming

Just below my feet they swim
Curling in and out of each other
They swim
Blood tears pain longing joys *faces*
Together here in this pool beneath my feet
They swim
The soles of my feet stir this water
And they swim
The window to everything
Just under the soles of my feet
I walk on this water
This seeps through my veins
How can I stand here
And tell you
What it is I feel
When it is everything?

Joy

My soul it skips and leaps
With joy
As a young unicorn born into
This day, my soul skips and leaps
For joy!
My spirit is not bound
My spirit is set free
Free and unstoppable
As the young unicorn
My spirit it skips
And leaps in joy
Unbound and free
And the Ἄλφά and Ὠμέγά
He gives to me a sceptre
A sceptre of opal and gold
He has made me a conqueror
My spirit unbound
My soul it skips
And I carry my sceptre
Of opal and gold
And I jump and skip
For joy

CLXXXIV

A Captain's Oath, The Words Of A Knight

We are all born the masters of our own shoreline; we're born on a shoreline and this shoreline belongs to us, we have an ocean in front of us that belongs to us, as well! This is our shoreline, and this is our ocean.

I have realized that for too long in my life, I have allowed people to extend their own shorelines far into mine, moving far inland, pushing my borders into a thin, almost-invisible etch and I have been standing in one spot for too long, afraid to move here, afraid to move there, for fear of stepping beyond these other people's borders! But I have learned that this is my shoreline, and that that is my ocean! These are my waves to master, my coast to rule and to reign! I have learned that my life consists of swimming in my ocean and digging up treasures (and burying treasures) on my land! Nobody has the right to move his or her own horizon beyond my horizon! They don't have the right to push their borders beyond my own! I will swim in my ocean, I will defend my land, I will build ships on my shore, fly in my sky, soar in my Heaven, and I will sail the ships that I build, I will sail into my waters! And when I want, I will swim! I will swim as much as I want!

I have this life, and while I have it, I'd better not let anyone try to impede on it, I'd better not let anyone attempt to conquer it, and I'd better not let anyone trespass into it! The horizons of others can only stretch as far into mine as I allow them to. The boundaries of other people can only reach as far beyond my own as I allow them to. I will start walking; I will not stay anymore in this one spot! And as I walk, their borders will shrink back, as I wade in the water, their boundaries will fall asea, and as I swim and sail and fly, they will have to accept their own realities while keeping themselves out of mine!

We are not born to rent out our coast, our shoreline, our sea, our ocean, our skies, our Heaven, we are not born as sacrifices! We are not born for the benefit of others, we are born for the benefit of ourselves. We are given this ocean for us to swim in, we are given this sky for us to fly into, we can plant trees, or we can cut trees! We can bury treasure or we can dig up treasure! We can construct bridges or we can destroy them! We can sail in ships or we can swim! We can fly with our wings or we can fly on our dreams! We can do anything we want to do, we can be anyone we want to be, we can be who we are. We can have what is ours, and we can keep it! We don't have to give it away.

I am going to be me, and I seek no shoreline to conquer, I seek no horizon to impede upon. I have my own! And no one can impose upon it; no one can desecrate me.

(This diary entry is borrowed from the novel: Dimensions, by C. JoyBell C.)

Consuming Fire

I was not gifted with patience and
I have no forbearance to remain here
Still and immoveable and untouchable
On this high steady breeze up here
Above the mountains I soar but I wait
For the drift to come For the winds to
Pick up direction under my wings

I have no patience to be still and steady
I am tired I am weary I am trapped
Why do you force this darkness out from me?
This darkness creeps out from me Leaks out from me
A steady drip, a constant falling, a sudden
combustion
This heat it burns within me on my flesh it
Scathes my skin and in my eyes I look with no mercy

The absence of mercy it overcomes me and
In an instant I become the carving
Blasted out from the rocky cliff with dynamite
Suddenly I walk with an ignited soul and
He who dares scorn me is given no mercy

CLXXXVIII

Why must it be this way? But this is what I am!
Send me a drift to catch my wings so I may be free!

So that this waiting will no longer provoke
the fire that consumes me...

A Tragedy

I think I caught
A glimpse
Of the whisper left
With you
The whisper that I
Left you
On the day when
You doubted

From the corner of
My eye
I see a feather
Laying there
A feather from my
Wing dropped
On the day when
You feared

On the edge of
My skin
I feel a teardrop
Your tear

CXC

Still warm but frozen
In time
On the day when
We lost

The whisper in your
Ear and
My feather on the
Ground and
Your tear somewhere near
My skin
On the day when
We fell

I hoped my soul
To whisper
For forever in your
Ear and
Cradle you in my
Wings and
Feel your every tear
But then…

…you stopped believing in angels

CXCI

Ugliness

A

Cryptic

Ugly

Grotesque

Hideous

Black

Ornament

Called

Doubt

The Dawn

On the ghostly mists
That float over the
Darkness of the shadows
Of a day that's past
Bloom and bud the
Blossoms of promise in
Tiny shining rays
Of light nourished by
The eternal soul *ànima eterna* and
As we stand at the
Cliff of a new day
Twilight will soon set in
All around us and
The tiny shining rays of
Blossoming promises will lead
Us home into the dawn
Of a new day

As the shadows of dusk fall
And rest all around us
At our feet
The birth of our brand new

Horizons reach forth and
Call us into and forward

Steady as she goes

Forward always forward

The Flight Of The Elfin Girl

Through the Nant Yr Arian running fast
She catches the flying four-leaf-clover
Her smile is broader than daylight and
The twinkle in her eye: star-brinked and
Reflected in the stars this night

The wind has winged her
As the moon snows clovers
The four-leaf one takes flight through
The Gwydyr Wood she drifts swiftly
On the winds to catch it!

The elfin girl

Her hair has caught sparks of fire
From the leftover dusts of the sun
Struck back to life by lightning bugs
Her ears point upwards to the night clouds
That speckle the starry *awyr* over the Irish Sea

Morning flute music of The Hill of Tara run with her
Hours before their time has come!

And the elfin girl has star-brinked eyes
The color of mischief
And wonder

Over the stream she leaps
She's caught the clover in a moonbeam!
And in the *golau'r lleuad* her skin kisses magic
Bathed in white and transparent calico
The elfin girl: celestial

Covered by skin, brought to life by grace
Exquisite and remarkable
The elfin girl free and wild
The elfin girl unleashed and uncaptured
This night we look at forever

A Thousand Jasmines Bloom

Take me and make me
All of yours
Into you
I find
My other half
Inside your eyes
I touch my soul
Take all of me
Before I am
Completely lost
Tired of being
A thousand pieces
Pick up the pieces of me
Gather me
Into your hands
Put me back together
In your palms
Where a thousand pieces lay
A thousand jasmines bloom
Broken
Yet unstoppable
The blossoming

Of a thousand jasmines
In your hands

Don't be afraid

This is all of me
In your palms
I come back together again
In your hands,
I am born of new breath
Look at me

Do not be afraid

Of a thousand jasmines blooming
Run outside
Let your hands bathe in the rain
Run outside
Let the moon awaken me
The blossoming of a thousand jasmines
Awaken me
And I shall be taken
Awaken me
And I shall be *forever yours*

CXCVIII

Inside Each Other

Today
I stand in
you
and you stand in
me.

I
no longer know where
I
begin and
where
you end or where you
begin
and where I end.

I stand in
you
and you stand in
me
your blood
is
my blood.

O'er The Hallway

Evening draws nigh o'er the hallways of doors, windows, and bridges.

I close no doors, I shut no windows, I burn no bridges.

Evening falls down o'er the hallway of doors, windows, and bridges.

And in the dark, sunbeams filter through my windows, sunshine dances through my doors, and truth gallops o'er my bridges.

Even as the evening sleeps heavily.

And sooner than soon, morning has come!

It Is Okay To Shine

I stepped into this world under a sunbeam.

The light was white and soft- like a dove.

It filtered through my eyes, my hair, my skin.

I looked beyond…it was only black and noisy.

But then they pulled me out into the dark and noise.

The dark and the noise were things I didn't know.

It hurt me.

I saw my sunbeam again; it came through my
window one morning.

I remembered.

They can't pull me out of my sunbeam- not ever
again.

Now the light filters through me again and again.

I glow a warm glow.

It is okay to shine.

I Wait For You

In the wee hours of the morning
Long before the sun will rise
This door I cannot shut
I stand in this door and wait

I wait for you I wait for you
My eyes will not close to rest
My heart will not be at peace
In the wee hours of the morning

Why do I believe you will come?
Why does my soul search for you?
In the darkness of these hours
In the solitude of this place

I wait for you I wait for you
Every morning long before the sun arises
I do not know why I should believe
I do not know in whom I believe

In whom do I believe to come?
For whom do I wait to arrive?

CCIII

In this door I stand alone
From in this door my eyes search

My eyes search for something they cannot see
My soul yearns for someone it does not know
I do not remember you but I wait
I wait for you I wait for you

From where do you come? From how far?

Who are you?

Who Is This Mortal?

I pulled up
The side of the blanket
Of stars
That covered the night
On my knees
The blanket of stars grazed my thigh
I looked down from above
Through the nights of the universe
The night was dark
The stars were many
Where
Is the absence of fear?
Is it under here?
Under the blanket of these stars?
I plucked the rays
Of the sun
They danced
The sun twirled
I turned every ray
Of the sun
Upside down
And I looked…

Where
Is the absence of fear?
Does it mix itself
Amongst the rays
Of the sun?
I ran
I skipped
I've tossed up my heels
Over the valleys
The streams
Of forever and ever
I've called out…
I have cried
Night after night
But she evades
Me
The absence of fear
Is not
Here
Where is she?
She lives not
In my abode
Where is she?
Cradled in the heart
Of a mortal man

She thrives
Give her to me
All of her
Now that I have found her
Within the heart
Of a mortal man
My faithful searching
Has come
To an end
My faithfulness
Has found
A resting place
A home
Where I once thought…
In a place
Where I once thought
I would never find
It
Down
Below
In the heart…
Bound up
In the heart
Of a mortal
Man

CCVII

Who is this mortal?

Give him to me

You and Me

In my castle
Of many rooms
And towers
The sun shines bright
And inside and outside
All of the world
Is for me

In my castle
Many rooms are locked
Many towers are chained
I've thrown away the keys
Never wanting to remember
For every day
The sunshine raptures me

In my castle
One day you stood
I saw you
You had all the keys
To all the rooms
To all the towers

CCIX

You found each key for me

In my castle
I stood-afraid
Where did you find those keys?
Must I go back?
What's behind those doors?
I have forgotten
Can't I just let the sunshine rapture me?

In my castle
You said "We must"
And then you walked towards the doors
You climbed the stairs
You lit the barren hallways
I followed close behind you
You led the way for me

In my castle
I remembered
Behind those doors
The fallen trees The cracked walls
The lost boats The drifting bottles
Then I remembered-yes I remembered
You held up the lantern for me

CCX

In my castle
Behind those doors
I looked at you
You took my hand
My tears fell down
As I remembered
Because you remembered for me

In my castle
Up in the towers
The dead leaves rustled beneath my feet
As I remembered
My tears fell down
I became broken better
You remade my heart for me

In my castle
Today no doors are locked
Today no towers are chained up
All the windows are open
I no longer wait
To be raptured by the sunlight
You rapture my heart for me

CCXI

In my castle
Every day
I learn something new
You teach me to remember
Every day
You remake my heart some more
You rebuild my heart for me

In my castle
Sometimes if I forget again
Promise me that you'll never
Promise me that you'll be
In the barren hallways
Carrying the keys
And lighting the way for me

Only Forever

There's a corner here
There's a sidewalk there
A stall over to the right
A road over to the left
I thought I saw you
Standing at the corner
But I want forever
I thought I saw you
Waiting down the road
But I want forever
We come
From so many places
We meet
At so many stops
We could walk away
With another in hand
But what is the point
If we don't want forever?
I thought I saw you
Smiling at me
I thought I heard you
Ask me

To wait at the bus stop
With you
Together
We could look at the sunbeams
Together
We could point at the stars
Together
We could buy cherry cola
But what is the point
If we don't want forever?

I want forever…
Only forever

All Of You With Dirty Hands

There is a never-ending moveable banquet
A table prepared for everyone
When thunder cracks open the clouds
That is the sound of it
Being pulled over the floor of the sky!
And everyone is welcome!
Everyone
From every city
And every nation
Every tribe, every tongue
The banqueting table moves
And all are called to come!
The black sits beside the white
The devout sits next to the atheist
Believers in one thing
Believers of nothing
Believers of many things
And those who are not sure
The free
The slave man
The king
The servant

All!

All are called to come

Come and sit!

We are all,

All of us are brothers and sisters!

We sit at this banqueting table prepared by His hands

The Alpha and Omega

The Beginning and the End

Calls us as one

He who does not need our belief

He who does not need the righteousness of man

He who graciously lays food upon our plates

And says Eat!

Eat! Every last one!

You are all brothers and sisters!

He who sees no stain, no flaw, no fear

He who looks not for holiness in man

Only those who have eyes for their own

righteousness

Cannot sit at this table

It is only they

Who will not come to this table!

They have no need for He who is I Am

They have no need for He who puts

Food on our plates

CCXVI

Without washing His hands!
They have no need for He who requires
Nothing of man
And counts their righteousness as filthy rags!
They have no need for He who only has eyes
For the righteousness of One Man- His Son
They have no need for a gift that is finished,
For a banquet that is said and done
But all of you!
All of you with dirty hands, come!
We need not wash our hands before we sup
At the never-ending
Moveable banquet

Miracle

It is like
A sweet, crimson poison
Drop by drop
Sweetly poisoning, deeply coloring
Every drop like a
Crimson cloud of mist dispersing
Steadily unfurling its wings
Like a scarlet angel

The scarlet angels fly
Slowly in my glass of water
Gliding, envenoming this water
Molecule upon molecule: a parasitism
Sweet crimson turns my water into wine
The overcoming I have long awaited

Let me transform Let me transform Let me
transform

From water into wine

CCXVIII

Grace

Behold the waterfall!
She springs forth!
Budding and sprouting
Like a deep spring of eternal waters
Breaking free to the surface of the earth
For the first time.
Fervently, Serenely, Calmly
Unstoppable, Fresh, Vibrant
The water breaks and buds forth
And falls from the crown of this cliff

Long stemmed roses of all colors
Burst forward in ferocious beauty and gentleness!
They merge together in torrents:
Long thornless stems crowned with brilliantly
colored petals!
Cascading as they do this fall, this downward dance
Down the drop, intertwined in water
A loose braid of aqua and long-stemmed roses
Erupting and dropping together
Imagination is void of the natural occurrence of this

Unnatural, Unlikely

Look again now!
The water has evaporated!
And left are the roses piled up like boulders!
In the parched stream that has run dry
Lie piles of thornless roses!
What is the meaning of this?
Unfading, everlasting roses on a thirsty ground?
Is the meaning of this I see, a frightful one?
This unnatural occurrence
This otherworldly reality
What is the meaning?

This is grace

You Can Find Me

You can find me
When you close your
Eyes and feel the
Breath that you are
Breathing in, hold
It to you closely and slowly
Exhale while your blood
Flows through your veins,
It swims in new
Oxygen; there you will
Find me as your
Mind stops racing as
You are in this
Place; only right here
From wherever you are
You can find me
Only if you stop
Stop and see me
Hear me whisper now
And you will see
And you will find
You can find me

Save Me

The black flies drop like
Charred sesame seeds
Through a funnel
Through the funnel of time
The ashen pestilence descends
Stripped
I have lost the plagues
I once identified
But alas!
They fall
Only to rise up again
Like an onyx ghost
A ghost built from
A million pieces
It rises again and
Falls again
Only to rise again!

Chaos

This is the true hell
Tartarus

I have never seen it
Hide me away!

Hide me away in the
Windows of my port
Where the stones meet the
Sea and the seagulls fly

Hide me away between
The door and the iron gate
Where the windows see the
Water and the seagulls fly

This pestilence
It haunts me

This noir wickedness
It falls and rises

Confusion

Into the rocks the steps the cliffs
Rising from the sea; the Liguria
Back to the eternal waters blue and green

CCXXIII

Where rock is swallowed by sea

Returning, I will sit in my window again
Where they cannot find me

Hide me

Where they cannot touch me
I want no part in this

Take me home

Save me

The Differents 2

Come with me on the flight
Of ten thousand seagulls, lets
Divide us among them and
Cascade on their wings
In the place where I come from
Far away from here
I used to sit and fly and float
Come with me and I could
Show you where ten thousand
Seagulls roam
They carry our souls to
Wherever we want to go!
And would you still come with me
To the place where it hurts, where
Their tears roll over our skin and
We feel all that is not our own
But is theirs
It becomes ours
To the place of sharing and
Would you stay to watch me
Dance inside their souls
And they dance into mine?

Would you stay if
You had to hear every thought
You had to see every pain
You had to feel every whisper
You would be always different
You say that I'm different but
Do you really know how different?

Sands

The sands of time
Rain onto my face
Trickling over my skin
Like a breeze
In sunshine
Quietly they rustle
Like autumn leaves
Skimming the edge of my body
Taking away from me
The minutes
The hours
The days
The moments
That I have left behind
And yet
Always with me
Never too far away

Sands.
Of time.
In the winds.
In sunshine.

CCXXVII

Sometimes A Bird

If I were a bird
I would breathe air
Through my limbs
And feast on sunlight
Through my eyes

If I were a bird
I would forget what's
Left down below
Take to the winds
Lifted by light

If I were a bird
My smile would be
The rippling seashore
My joys would be
The ocean foams

Turquoise

If I were a bird
I'm not sure if

CCXXVIII

I'd bring you
With me or if
I'd just float

If I were a bird
I couldn't say if
I'd take you
With me or if
I'd just fly

Fly

Eating A Grape

The red juice curls off the corners of her lips
Dripping, oozing down the edge of her chin
Her eyes slowly close
Her long thick ebony lashes skim the top of
Her alabaster skin
And the tastes and the thoughts and
Even the soft plucking sound of the
Harvest of the grapes play on her
Tongue
The rough hands that picked the
Fleshy textured pulp of grape in her mouth
Seem to run their fingers over her lips
The taste of the sun burning on the surface of
The thin red transparent skin dusted
By the vineyard winds sweeping up from
Dirt ground
The rustling of the leaves on the vines
Tastes of the sunburned skin tilled by warm winds
The low low low soft thud of the
Bunches dropped into beige baskets
Smells of sweat-stained shirts clinging to
Hard-worn backs bronzed by the *sol*

Sweet scents of lost fruit trodden underfoot

She swallows

The tender white whispers of the morning *luz del sol*
Stains the ivory walls of her bedroom

The ivory China bowl
The red grapes

The motion of her fingertips plucking
A single one
Like a secret so silent that no one
Has ever told

And the grape touches her lips again...
Her opaque lashes lower and bow...

All over again...

A Vision of Yellow

I caught a glimpse of the yellow
From the corner of my eye
The heat in the air transcending;
Melting my vision- smouldering it
Into the surrounding
Like a burnt Polaroid
Wait; then I look beyond
In all cognizance
I see the trains on the tracks
The static and mobility
But here all has stopped
Right here where I am; where
The yellow catches my eye
The yellow stops me and
The stones gently rolled and
Not-so-sharp; they are seared
Into this momentary existence here
The heat mixes everything together
Here in this mirage
Of yellow tulips and small stones
It is very hot
The trains and tracks surround me

CCXXXII

In the train station

Nobody sees the yellow tulips- only me

Aeternum

And the silhouette of three red roses outlined against
the cashmere Appearance of her ivory skin
Casts shadows like the doubts of spiritual songs sung
in the Basilicas While the etches of renegade strands
of her hazel hair blissfully mark the Lines of reason
and meaning for life and of eternal things
And as she breathes, her wistful locks sway like paper
birds Hanging in the wind Born anew like the
constant morning peaking through as sunlit rays
Of infinite sunbeams that have met the eyes of all our
predecessors And the angels and the demi-gods
For all of this I see the worth of worship, why they
worshipped her She who was carved by the hands of
God; If color did not exist in the world
And she were but a statue of marble or a sculpture
cast in white cement Still she would rise and stand
monumental, glistening in the sunshine! Above all
the rest And if she were a sculpture hidden in the
dark corners of a galleria The fingerprints of God
marked all over her figure would call out to all the
Blood of life rushing through every passerby and

imprint the epidermis of the Almighty onto each
person deep inside their souls

Thus, she can never be forgotten
And she never was

The Goddess

These dark waves have rolled over
My face before
I have been here before
Baptized in these rushing waters
The night is velvet and ebony and I
Think I should be feeling lost but I
Feel like I am here again
In the dead of night
In these indigo waters
Rolling with the ocean's current
Being too familiar I am not lost
But being too far away I am
Afraid to be lost
And is this a place I've come from?
From the midnight waters was I born?
And is this a place I return to
When my soul remembers?
These waves they know me too well
This current pulsates
My bloodstream
The rush in my ears:
Music

From somewhere I have always known

The Vision In The Castle Gates
(Castello di Portovenere)

I will run through these roads
Where they cannot find me
Through these narrow paths
And up these stone stairways
Doors and windows
Steps and stairs
Visions of old men
And children
Stain the corners of my eyes
As I run
I hear their laughter
As I run
I think I see someone
I remember
But I've never seen before
As I run
My spirit picks up flight

Look at her she spins
Through these narrow paths
Shadows blurry all around her

CCXXXVIII

All has become but a shadow
That surrounds her
Her heels pick up flight
She looks to left
And to the right and
She spins, she looks at us
Like she almost remembers
Then she goes
The vision

The smells of food and wine
The colors of gelato
These stones
These cobblestones
I will touch these walls and
I will feel these stones on
The bottoms of my feet
All is a ghost
All is one ghost
Whom I breathe in and out
This smell of food
This sound of laughter
This stone under my touch
This heals me
I am healed

CCXXXIX

Look at this vision before us!
Where has she come from?
She steals the ghosts
Of our pasts
And dances in our aromas
What is left but only
The melting of the senses
Nothing but air
All is gone
She has eaten everything
She dances in our
Ancient shadows

All that's past is mine
All that's now and that's tomorrow
I will leave not one drop of
This wine for the taking
I will lick the streams of *vino*
From off these beaten tables
And leave nothing
All is mine
Ascending to the castle

CCXL

The Water

The boat has turned around the ocean's bend
Come from the winter's snow and cold winds
The man sits in front of me and rows
This ocean's bend is different
Winter has been left behind and
I see turquoise
White stones piled up; an underwater plateau rises
From the bottom of this shallow *mer*
The winter gone has broken way for our boat and
These *aguamarina* waters are still
These blue-green waters are silent
So silent I can feel it
I can feel the serenity of these *turchese* waters
Penetrate my skin; my soul swims
And the man rows steady now; steady and quiet
His oar strikes into the deep blue of the beyond and
I look ahead to where we are going
A sapphire blue, saturated, farther and farther
Away until the vastness races towards the skies!
White winter Shallow turquoise Sapphire depth
And we sail

It is not about the man; he is only rowing
It is not about the boat; I can walk on water
But it is about the water…

It is changing

You Can't Catch Me!

Did you not know?
That my soul has wings
Bigger than your wings
And I take flight?
In the night and
In the daylight and
Right below your nose
I take flight and
I do not care of
Your formalities and
Your hypocrisies and
Your bondages and
Chains
Did you not know?
Right below your nose
I take flight and
My wings are far
Bigger than your wings!

The Scent Of A Man

Rough skin colored by the sun
Under my fingers feels like
Sand on the oceans' shores

Strong arms like twin pillars
Beneath my palms feel like
Marble towers of forgotten pasts

The tendons in his neck
Turn his face towards me like
The steady strength of fortresses

and

Under his skin my sweat is born
Between his arms my breaths are stolen
His neck is where my kisses burrow

Oh the scent of a man…
For the lingering scent of a man
The whole world does pale in comparison!

CCXLIV

Firenze

The streets of Florence are like labours of love
And walking on them like walking on the backs of
A hundred and thirty sweaty men toiling in the sun

There is a heaviness which drapes the air in Florence
A sweet deception I have likened unto thick,
enigmatic oil paints
Disanimated on the tops of canvases

A viscous, sweetened poisoning drifts
in the winds of Florence
At first the taste is bitter but the aftertaste is
sweetened
The conditioning of one's senses like falling into a
trap

A lullaby which lulls the brightest man to sleep
The alleys of Florence like a drug painful and then
soothing
Her people walk in a daze; a saccharine enchantment

Florentines drunken on her thickened syrup like a
liquor
Each day the glories of a faded Renaissance relived
Every day the same day is played over again!

The laughter and the music The wind and the cheers
They are but reruns of the past caught forever
Within our dimension; the ghosts replay themselves

Walk, walk, walk and walk and walk looking down
Down on the Florentine cobblestones past Via
Signoria
Her beauty cannot be denied but alas cannot be
lived!

La Città Eterna

I stand here
My map in hand
A thousand people
Or more
On every side and all around me
Yet I know not one face

The sky is eternal
The skies of the Eternal City
Loom and swell
Up above me
And the cobblestone under my feet is hot
I have never been here before

I know not one face
Nor any one street
I have never been here before
And yet
Here inside of me I have come home
I have come back home!

And the sun blazes in the never- ending skies
Of La città eterna

CCXLVII

Time stops
It is frozen
All around me and I sit Enthroned

In this moment now

Right here Right now

With me

This is eternity

On this cobblestone,
The rocks seeth under the noon sun
At this corner
Near that fountain
Under this stop light
I am lost

And yet
I am found

CCXLVIII

Fontana di Trevi

Horses they rise up
From the waters and
One rides the calm
One rides the storms
Maestoso Incredibile Spettacolare
Bellissima
Carved marble Carved by
Demi-gods and angels
Her virgin waters spray
Through the air on
My face My skin
Breathe the virgin waters

Fontana di Trevi

An Amore

(June 15, 2010 ~ Roma, Italia)

The water glass breaks
It shatters
It falls to the floor
The little boy dropped the water glass
He broke it
Up here on the floors
Of the rooftop garden
I hear no screams of anger
No mad defamations
I hear no cries, no sorrowful explanations
Only cheers and gales of laughter
The little boy runs around
Again he breaks another
Glass after glass falls down
Not an angry look is cast
Not a single angry word
Glasses shatter
Voices cheer
"Amore! Amore! Mamma mia, Amore!"
Is all that I hear!

I remember the water glass

CCL

That I broke as a girl
And the next one
And the next one
I still feel the stinging
Of all those angry words
The broken glasses caused me
The spankings
The furious faces!

But here in Roma…

All I hear is "Amore!"

Tears threaten
To overflow
My heart
To overcome me…

Oh! If only I lived in Roma!
I would be an amore!

Ten Thousand Years

These eyes…
Where have I seen them before?
Never have I seen them before
Yet
I know these eyes
I know this soul
Is it from a dream?
For if so…
It must have been a very long dream
Did I dream a dream
For a thousand long years?
It's you…
Your eyes…
Where have I seen them before?
Never have I seen them before
Yet
I know your eyes
I know you
Did we skip and play together as children?
For if so…
Perhaps I was always a child
And always will be a child

Because then and now
Are both right here together
In your eyes
Is it you?
It is you!
But from where…
I seem to have forgotten…
Was it long, long ago
In a land far away?
Is it my tomorrow?
Is it my today?
Is it my yesterday?
I know you…
Yes…
I do know you…
Somehow…
I feel I have looked into your eyes
Every moment
For the past ten thousand years!
Chills run over my skin
With every drop of blood in me
I know you too well
From the foundations of the face of the earth
From the time
When time began

CCLIII

I know you…
Until the stars in the sky are fallen
Until we are one with the angels
Until the time
When time is no more
I will know you

There is no time
There is no beginning
There is no end

I know you
You are mine
I am yours

You will never lose me

The Return

On my journey, I have learned that…

Nothing is definite, there is no black and white. Everything is to you as you see it; if you want to take a plainsketch paper and color the lines in with bright red-like blossoms in the gardens that smell so sweet, then you may! But it doesn't have to always be bright red! You can flood your blank papers with red today, then blue tomorrow, and then if you want, after that, you can color them purple, violet, pink– you can change everything by changing the way you see it! By changing the colors.

I have learned that the best thing to do is what you want to do and if you don't know what it is that you want to do– just start walking in one direction and if that's the direction you want to go, you'll find that you will keep on going. But if it's not really where you want to go, you'll find yourself turning around and going where you really want to!

I have learned not to look for the "right thing" because life is not about looking for "what's right." It's about looking for *what's yours*.

I have learned that there is nothing to be afraid of, really! And if you say "I can do it," you can! Really.

I have learned that crossing the street isn't too hard, and that it's okay for your feet to get dirty sometimes.

I have learned that Destiny is real. I've learned what she is, and how she works.

I have learned that it is possible to fall in love in a few days.

I have learned that seagulls are beautiful and that they are like white paper planes floating through the sky with bells attached to them!

I have learned that there are too many wonderful people in the world to waste my time thinking of the no-good ones.

The world is bigger than you think it is, and it is perfect. The good and the bad, the black and the white, together it is all perfect. Gray is perfect.

So there is nothing to be afraid of.

Really.

This is what I have learned.

If I Could Taste You

Like
Sweet
Dew
Drops
Of
Sugar
From
The
Cane

On
My
Tongue

With
My
Eyes
Closed

Tonight I Pray

Alone
And under the stars
Beneath this big glass window
I sit
Looking to the sky
The night
Sky up above me
My lantern…
The flame…
Casts shadows all around me
All is silent
One and all
Are asleep
Yet my breath
Raises
To the heavens
In silent whispers
To God above
"Oh God guide me"
The lantern…
The flame…
Casts dancing glows

Before my eyes
"Oh heavenly hosts of God
Hold onto me
Angels in heaven above
And all around me
Do not forsake me"
My whispers
My prayers
Raise
Into the night's sky
They reach
Beyond the stars
Into the heavens
Where they echo
Resounding
They echo
My prayers
To God
And all His heavenly hosts
Above
In heaven
All is silent
One and all
Are asleep
Only my whispers

My prayers
My angels surround me
Gabriel, Michael
Raphael, Barachiel
God in heaven
He sees me
He will answer me
He hears my prayers
He will answer me
The heat of
The lantern…
The flame…
On my brow
Casts beads of sweat
As my prayers
Fervently rise
To the heavens
Above me
"Oh God hear me
Do not forsake me"
My whispers
My prayers
All is silent
One and all
Are asleep

Only the sound
Of my breath
Is resounding
In whispers
In prayers
To God above
And all His angels
All around me
Tonight
I pray
"Oh God
Show me
Where fear
Is not
Show me
The absence of fear
Show me"
Tonight
I pray

Like A Dove

There you stand
Your armor glistens
In the sunlight
Your sword sharp
Sharp as death
But your eyes
Are soft like
A dove's eyes

And you call
Call to me
And you say
Come to me
Meet me here
Where I am
In my armor
With my sword

Here I am
In my tower
And they say
There is no

Knight in armor
And they say
Knights are dead
Knights are buried

But you call
Call to me
And your armor
Glistens in sunlight
Your sword sharp
Sharp as death
Your eyes soft
Soft like doves

I will come
Come to you
Meet you there
In your armor
Arisen from death
No grave holds
My own knight
Knight in armor

From my tower
I will descend

CCLXIV

All the voices
Say you're naught
That you're dead
That you're buried
That there's no
Knight in armor

But I cross
Cross the bridge
I will cross
Cross the lake
I will run
Run to you
Your dove eyes
Call to me

Soft like breath
I am here
I will go
Go with you
From this tower
From this bridge
From this lake
Take me away

CCLXV

Your heart soft
Soft like doves
The air perfect
Perfect like morning
On your horse
We ride away
The voices lie!
You are real

Worthy

The little girl dances
In circles and she sings
In circles there she goes
She laughs and laughs
Her emeralds glisten
Heavily laden with jewels
She glistens
And her crown
Upon her head
It towers
A towering crown of rubies
Only a little girl
But unto her all
Is given
And she knows
Her worth

An End Birthing a Beginning

I feel as though
I have hit the end
And will go on into my new beginning

I feel as though
The mercurial waters rush
Underneath my feet these silver waters race

At this gleaming new horizon
The *acqua* does not flow into it
The sky does not fall into it;

The silver waters and the sky and the
Colors of the sunset flow away
And into what has past

For at this new horizon
Exists nothing that is finished
But only all that is new

Time and space

CCLXVIII

Come and go
I am here always

I will step in to this new horizon
I will let the old waters flow away
I will allow the old sky to slip through my fingers

The mercurial waters race
And I will enter into this new place
Something new awaits me
Something new calls my name
Open arms they wait for me
I leave all the tears in old lakes

Only joy uncontained
Only dreams fulfilled
Only happiness, only love

Here goes my first step

CCLXIX

It

Rising from ground below sea level
A buried tower crushed and forgotten
Emerging again; ascending from the ashes
Aiming with its peak towards the skies
Pointing up and forward as the
Sunlight and the raindrops cleanse
The dried mud cracking and
Falling and dripping from its body

Arisen from the dead like a transparent white
Phoenix ablaze with translucent fire
Stretched forth and reaching
Grabbing and grasping for breath
Eyes clear as the sun
Pupils fixated
In a forward surge it lunges
Towards the Heavens and
Sheds its many feathers
They snow onto the ground they
Flake into the air they
Shed and drift to the ground
In the air

CCLXX

They are left behind as it
Ascends it
Lunges it
Unravels up and
Forward
Pressing
Through the air it expands the troposphere

Emerging from the waters like
A human without breath
It thrusts,
Pierces through the twilight air
And inhales
Lungs expanded
Moonlight bathes its
Skin, hair
Water abandons these streams
Of moonlight on this skin
Leaving nothing behind
Taking all and falling
Off of this skin like
The shedding of all falsities

It
Is here

CCLXXI

It
Has taken place

My incarnation

Heaven

The sun has an ocean.

An ocean so deep, vast
and blue.

And on these eternal waters I float.

And while I float, I can hear the
seagulls nearby.

Heaven has come down to earth
for me.

A Dream

I have a dream,
and in my dream,

the sunlight

is snowing,

and on the snow
are many lights and

all is warm in

the sunlight's snow.

And the sun snows
just for me.

Angel

His eyes are beautiful and frightened
Black and white
His wings are soaked in rain
Feathers clinging low onto the rocks
Frightened like a newborn bird
Soaked in rain
His hair is black
His skin like marble
Black and white
On the vehement ground
His hands press onto the jagged rocks
Hands and feet
He perches
Like a bird positioned for flight
But he is frightened
And all is black and white
On this rocky ocean shore
The waves rage
At the son of the sea
The waters have borne a winged one
Frightened Alone
Hostile Cold

Come with me, angel
I will not leave you
Come with me, angel
I will protect you
Come with me
You are hostile
And cold
Come with me
Stay with me
I will protect you

Anticipation

I am
Poisoned and lovestricken
With the
Thick, thick fluids
Of
Anticipation
They ooze like
Apple tree sap
Like
Lava
Hot lava
I anticipate
Burning bright
And poisoned
With
Anticipation

CCLXXVII

The End

I'm not in search of sanctity, sacredness, purity;

these things are found after this life, not in this life;

but in this life I search to be completely human: to

feel, to give, to take, to laugh, to get lost, to be

found, to dance, to love and to lust, to be so human.

Thank You...

Thank *you*, whoever you are, for reading all the way to the end! I feel that you have been with me on a secret journey and have become my apprentice in magic! My wish is that my words will become a part of you for the rest of your life, and that it will then be something that you can hand down to your children, and to their children, all the way down to your great-grandchildren! Thank you for reading the things that I write!

In the past, I have thanked so many individuals on the acknowledgment pages of my books but now I realize how unnecessary that is. Moreover, how fast people change! So, if you love me and care for me now, and plan to stay that way, I thank you! If you support my writings and read what I write, I thank and cherish you. If you hold me in high esteem and if I am valuable to you, I thank you! *A viaxe continúa*!

Notes...

Notes...

The main typeface in this book is set in 14 pt.
Perpetua, by Eric Gill (1882- 1940) who was a British
sculptor and stonecutter named *Royal Designer for
Industry* by the *Royal Society of Arts* in London. The
font itself was made to resemble hand-chiseled
engravings, hence, who better to create such a feel
for a font, than a sculptor and stonecutter?

"Perpetua may be judged in the small sizes to have
achieved the object of providing a distinguished form
for a distinguished text; and, in the large sizes, a
noble, monumental appearance."

~ Stanley Morison

CPSIA information can be obtained at www.ICGtesting.com
Printed in the USA
LVOW13s1935220813

349189LV00001B/39/P